OUTDOOR ART

by Teresa Heapy

OXFORD
UNIVERSITY PRESS
AUSTRALIA & NEW ZEALAND

OXFORD
UNIVERSITY PRESS

Oxford University Press is a department of the University of Oxford.
It furthers the University's objective of excellence in research,
scholarship, and education by publishing worldwide. Oxford is a registered
trademark of Oxford University Press in the UK and in certain other countries.

Published in Australia by
Oxford University Press
Level 8, 737 Bourke Street, Docklands, Victoria 3008, Australia

ISBN 9780190318376

Series Editor: Nikki Gamble
Designed by Oxford University Press in collaboration with Fiona Lee, Pounce Creative
Printed in Singapore by Markono Print Media Pte Ltd
Links to third party websites are provided by Oxford in good faith and for information only.
Oxford disclaims any responsibility for the materials contained in any third party website referenced in this work.

Acknowledgements

The publishers would like to thank the following for the permission to reproduce photographs:

p3: Babukatorium/Solent News/REX; **p4**: Kuttelvaserova Stuchelova/Shutterstock; **p5l**: Angelo Hornak/Alamy; **p5r**: Simon
Wallett; **p6–7**: Jennifer Turpin & Michaelie Crawford; **p7r**: Jennifer Turpin & Michaelie Crawford; **p8l&r**: Paul Mayall
Australia/Alamy; **p9b**: Ludovic Maisant/Hemis/Corbis; **p9t**: Navin Mistry/Alamy; **p10–11**: B Lawrence/Alamy; **p12–13**:
Marcio Jose Sanchez/AAP Photo; **p13r**: Topham Picturepoint/Topfoto; **p14–15**: Tim Roberts; **p15r**: Olivier Parent/Alamy;
p16: Snowball in Trees, 1980 (cibachrome print), Goldsworthy, Andy (b. 1956)/British Council Collection/The Bridgeman
Art Library; **p17**: Ice Arch, 1984 (cibachrome photos), Goldsworthy, Andy (b. 1956)/Leeds Museums and Galleries (Leeds
Art Gallery) U.K./The Bridgeman Art Library; **p18**: Tetra Images/Corbis; **p19b**: Smuay/Shutterstock; **p19m**: Kuttelvaserova
Stuchelova/Shutterstock; **p20b**: Hero Images/Getty Images; **p20t**: Blend Images/Alamy; **p21**: Tang Chiew Ling; **p22**: Tomas
del amo/Alamy; **p23m**: Clemente do Rosario/Alamy; **p24**: Simon Wallett. Background photos by Tanchic/Shutterstock;
Evgeny Karandaev/Shutterstock; Elenamiv/Shutterstock; Siro46/Shutterstock; Itsra Sarprasert/Shutterstock; Antpkr/
Shutterstock; Ensuper/Shutterstock; Nomad_Soul/Shutterstock; Ruskpp/Shutterstock Lora liu/Shutterstock; Jeka84/
Shutterstock; Vierra/Shutterstock.

Front & back cover photograph by Craig Roberts/Getty Images
Back cover photo by Topham Picturepoint/Topfoto

We have made every effort to trace and contact all copyright holders before publication. If notified, the publisher will
rectify any errors or omissions at the earliest opportunity.

Contents

Outside, Not Inside!

Sometimes we go to see works of art inside, in museums or art galleries. But you can also find art outside, in unexpected places – and you can make outdoor art yourself, too!

You can find pieces of art in the world around you. You can look at them from far away or you can get up close to them. Sometimes you can even touch outdoor art. Outdoor art could be a sculpture on the side of a building or a beautiful pattern of leaves.

A work of art is something creative that someone has made. It can express something about them, their life or where they live, or it could be something that springs from their imagination.

Winged Figure by Barbara Hepworth

Lovely Leaves, made by Libby (age 10) and Flo (age 7)

This work of art is made of metal, so its shape won't change and it will last a long time.

This work of art is temporary – this means it will not last for long. The circle will change as the leaves crinkle and dry up, and as the wind blows them around.

Think about it.

Do these works of art make you:

- look at the world in a different way?
- think about different images or stories?
- think about how you could make your own works of art?

5

City Art

Some artists make outdoor works of art in cities.

Being Outside

An outdoor work of art will change in the weather. It gets covered with snow. It shines in the sun. It gets blown around in the wind. It's always changing. And most importantly, when art is outside, lots of people can see it – and they don't have to pay!

This is called *Halo*. It's a large metal ring which keeps spinning around a tall silver mast. The ring looks like it might fall off ... but it never does! It's perfectly balanced. It moves with the wind and makes wonderful shadows in the sun.

Halo was made by Jennifer Turpin and Michaelie Crawford, and is in Central Park in Sydney.

This is called *Tied to Tide*. It was also made by Jennifer Turpin and Michaelie Crawford. It's made of planks of wood and some ladders! It is in Sydney Harbour. The ladders move in the waves and the wind. Sometimes the ladders spin around in a full circle!

Surprising Art

Antony Gormley is a sculptor. He makes metal statues of people and puts them outside in lots of different places. People are surprised and excited when they see them!

This is called *Inside Australia*. It's made up of 51 sculptures that are spread out a long way from each other. This outdoor artwork is in a very shallow salt lake that is around one million years old.

Inside Australia is in Lake Ballard, Western Australia.

Broken Column is made up of 23 figures all over the city of Stavanger in Norway. There are statues on a football field, beside the water and in a petrol station!

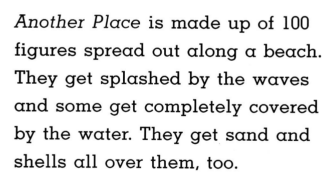

This statue is part of *Broken Column*.

Another Place can be seen in Crosby, England.

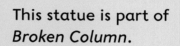

Another Place is made up of 100 figures spread out along a beach. They get splashed by the waves and some get completely covered by the water. They get sand and shells all over them, too.

The statues look like they're thinking ... what could they be thinking about?

Enormous Art

This statue by Antony Gormley is called *The Angel of the North*, and it's huge! It is as tall as four double-decker buses.

The statue's wings – from one end to the other – are almost as long as a jumbo jet. It's near a very busy road, so it's seen by over 90000 drivers every day!

This statue is made of steel and it took almost six months to build. About 700 tonnes of concrete and 32 tonnes of steel were used to help anchor the statue and keep it standing. The concrete and steel stretch 20 metres down below the surface of the ground. This huge statue won't fall over, even in very strong winds!

The Angel of the North is in Gateshead, England.

"The point about this work is that it has been built by a lot of people for a lot of people."

Antony Gormley

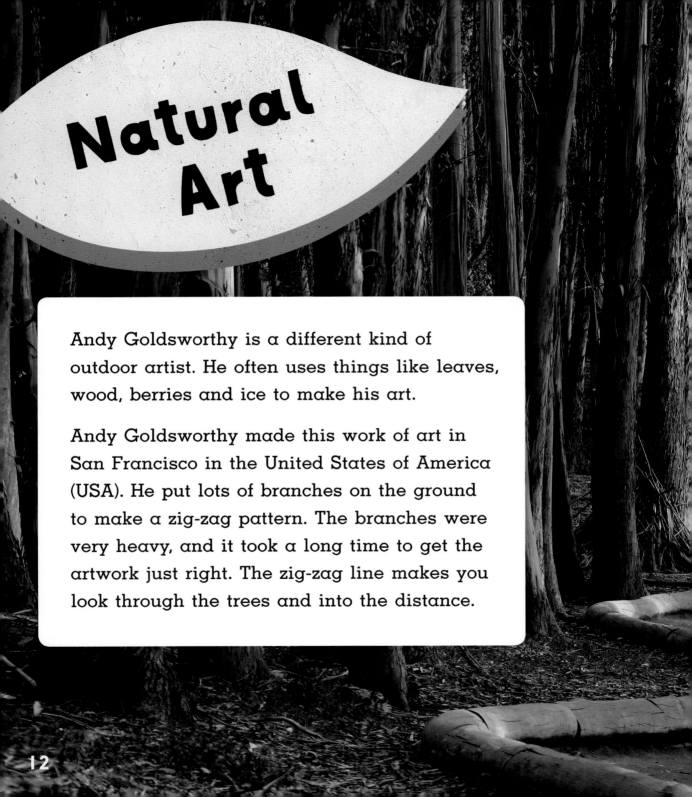

Natural Art

Andy Goldsworthy is a different kind of outdoor artist. He often uses things like leaves, wood, berries and ice to make his art.

Andy Goldsworthy made this work of art in San Francisco in the United States of America (USA). He put lots of branches on the ground to make a zig-zag pattern. The branches were very heavy, and it took a long time to get the artwork just right. The zig-zag line makes you look through the trees and into the distance.

For this work of art, Goldsworthy collected lots of leaves and carefully creased them. Then he laid them in a circle on the ground. He used thorns to hold them in place. When the sun shone on the leaves, the creases helped to make shadows.

Sometimes Andy Goldsworthy's art doesn't last very long. The wind, rain and sun can all change it. The leaves in this artwork wouldn't have looked like this for long – leaves become dry and brown in the sun and they curl up.

Long-lasting Art

Sometimes Andy Goldsworthy makes permanent works of art. He used granite and slate to make this pile of rocks, known as a cairn.

At the top of the cairn, he has planted a tree called a Strangler fig. One day, the Strangler fig will grow roots all the way down the sculpture. Strangler fig trees can live for hundreds of years, so this sculpture will keep changing for a very long time.

Strangler Cairn is in Conondale National Park in Queensland.

a Strangler fig tree

Weather Art

You don't think you can make outdoor art when the weather is bad? Think again! Sometimes the weather can *help* you make works of art! Other times it can make art disappear …

What do you think is going to happen to this snowball? How long do you think it will last?

Andy Goldsworthy used ice to make this amazing arch. He put a pile of stones in the middle, to hold up the ice. Then he left it to freeze into shape overnight, before carefully taking out the stones. There was a herd of cows in the field that could have knocked it down – but luckily they didn't! The arch only lasted a short time, but that makes it even more special.

Goldsworthy tried four times to make *Ice Arch* in Cumbria, England. The first three arches melted or fell down!

Your Own Outdoor Art

You can make outdoor art anywhere you like! You can use *anything* you find, too – you don't need paper and pens!

Plan it.

Think about what you want to create. You could get an idea from things you find outside. You don't have to be in a forest or a park – you can find leaves and sticks as you walk along the street.

Talk about it.

Go outside and look at what's around you. Talk to someone about the colours or textures you can see. What season is it? What's the weather like?

Collect it.

Collect leaves, sticks, petals, stones or berries that catch your eye. Try to only collect things that have fallen to the ground. Be careful though – some plants are poisonous, or sharp!

Use everything you've found to make different shapes such as circles, squares and spirals. You could make animal shapes, too! The sun can help you make shadows with different objects. You can stick things together with mud and grass. There are so many different things you can do!

Sometimes you don't need much to make art. You could just find some leaves and arrange them on the grass, or make shapes with stones on the beach ... and you've made a work of art!

Story Art

Sometimes you only need some leaves to make a picture – or even to make a whole story! Start by finding a few leaves. They can be green and bendy, or brown and crunchy.

Place one leaf on a blank piece of paper. Now think about all the things that leaf could be. Take a pen and draw some lines or people to make a picture. You could join different pictures together and make up a story about them.

This art was created by Tang Chiew Ling. She is an artist who makes pictures using things she finds around her.

a boat

someone wind-surfing

a rain cloud

Leaving Your Art

If you make a work of art outside, you can't take it with you – you will have to say goodbye to it.

Have you ever made a sandcastle and left it at the beach? It's a bit like that. Try to go back and see your art another day. Is it still there? Has it changed? Has it been moved – by animals, people, the wind or the sea? Has it been rained on or baked by the sun?

If your art is made of leaves or flowers, have they changed colour? Has that made your artwork better or worse?

Saying goodbye ... and hello!

When you say goodbye to your outdoor art, think about the people who might find it next. What will they think? They will probably be excited to find it. Your art is like a present from you ... to the next person who sees it!

Your special art

Don't forget to keep looking around you for ideas. Every day, each thing you find and each place you see will be different. Anything you make will be your own different and very special piece of outdoor art!

Index

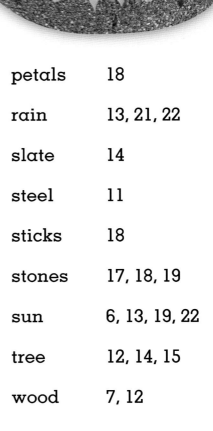